Superstition Mountains

The Mountains of Legend, Gold, Mystery, and Death

Matt Kincaid

ISBN: 9781795445184

Printed in the United States

MAPLEWOOD
PUBLISHING

Contents

Introduction

The Wild West has always been a place of fascination for both Americans and the rest of the world looking in on American culture. The idea of a cowboy is about as American as things can get, and the gunslingers of western films have been childhood heroes since before the talkies. Stories have been passed down about how the West was won, what sort of villains lurked between crags of rock on the slopes of dust-colored mountains, and how it looked as a cavalry of cowboys stormed across the plains underneath an endless blue sky and a blazing sun.

But there is more mythology to it than that, and a spirituality that is much older than any settlement or gold claim in the west. What appeared to settlers from the east to be wild and mesmerizing terrain had been home to native tribes for thousands of years. To them this land was their home, it was sacred, and they had their own stories to tell about it long before the heroes and villains of the Wild West swooped in with their guns blazing.

Of course, whenever cultures merge, their stories blend and their spirituality becomes intertwined—and that phenomenon was never more pronounced than in the Superstition Mountains in the central portion of Arizona.

The mountains loom over the valley that holds the Phoenix metropolitan area, standing like stone guardians of both the lowland and its secrets. Stories and traditions abound about what happens in the mountains, the mysteries to be found there, and the spirits both human and demonic that guard and haunt the hills. It's like something out of a storybook, but it's based not

1

on some scribbler's fevered imagination but on decades and centuries of events and people that could never quite be explained.

The story as we know it is this: There is a mountain range in the wilderness of Arizona that was the setting of native lore about the creation of the world, flood myths, and the origin of evil. All these stories center on the Superstition Mountains, which seem to have a strange hold over the psyches of those who live beneath their towering height.

Later, as the California Gold Rush spilled over into Arizona, the Superstitions attracted the attention of miners. Several mines existed in the general area, but the focal point of the legends was owned by the Peralta family. After they sold the land to a German immigrant named Jacob Waltz, he died suddenly—leaving behind cryptic clues about the greatest gold deposit in North America. Treasure hunting mania followed.

Are the legends true? That's the question everyone always asks about any legend. That's the very nature of a passed-down story. We know, in this one, that there are at least grains of truth. We know of the Peralta family; they served as governors of the New Mexico region. We know that Jacob Waltz was a real person. We know that many of the deaths associated with the mine really happened. We know, from newspaper clippings and other verifiable sources, that some sort of legends about the mine existed from the earliest days after Waltz's death.

This is a story where fact and fiction merge and mesh until sometimes it's nearly impossible to tell the difference. But that's what makes for some of the greatest stories! This book is not meant as a field guide or an encouragement to go treasure hunting yourself. It's a place to find some information about one of the greatest legends of the American southwest. It's a book that simply scratches the surface of all there is to learn about this legend and this place. Perhaps it will encourage you to do more research on your own.

Gold in America

Much of America's history is tied to the fervor for gold that led European settlers to the New World in the first place. All the way back in the 16th century, Hernan Cortez landed in Hispaniola (present-day Haiti and the Dominican Republic). His eventual march into the interior of Mexico would become the stuff of tragedy and the stuff of legend. While Cortez was looking for treasure of any kind, his fabled quest for gold—in fact, for an entire City of Gold—became a common piece of folklore surrounding his march to the Aztec capital. Conquistadors ranged into South America and Sir Walter Raleigh scoured Virginia, all in pursuit of the mythic El Dorado that was said to be located somewhere on the vast, unknown continent.

While it's geologically true that portions of the new continents were extraordinarily rich in gold, something less easily found across the sea in Europe, the idea of hidden treasures became something of a religion for many. The legends began with the Muisca people of Colombia, a lesser known ancient civilization from the American Mesopotamia who were as advanced as the Aztecs and Mayans. They placed a special significance on the color of gold, considering it to be the color of energy and creation. The most spectacular of their stories is that of the zipa (tribal chief) who would cover himself in gold dust and then wash it off in a lake while attendants threw more golden treasures into the water. The Spanish invaders took particular interest in these treasures and the myths surrounding them. The veracity of these myths remains something of a mystery; ancient maps depict the lake in question, but modern archeologists are still struggling to find the exact location and proof of its existence.

Still, for the European invaders and colonists, gold became the theme of this brave new world. Gold mania would often fade into the background, but the idea of gold hidden in this strange land continued to hold the imagination of the growing American public. It was all tied, of course, to the dream of getting rich quick. The American Dream, if unattainable by the favored means of hard work and industry, might be achieved by luck if you happened to stumble upon a vein of gold, stake a valid claim—and avoid getting killed for it.

The Treaty of Guadalupe Hidalgo at the conclusion of the Mexican-American War officially transferred the land that would become California into the hands of the United States government in 1848. The gold rush began in January of the same year with a well-timed, accidental discovery by a foreman at Sutter's Mill in Coloma, a small town north of San Francisco. James Marshall, who worked for John Sutter, discovered a shiny piece of metal in the water wheel of the mill. He brought his find to his boss, and when the two quietly tested the metal they found that it was genuine gold. They agreed to keep the discovery quiet because Sutter hoped to establish an agricultural empire in the West and did not want to see his plans derailed by a mad rush for gold. However, it took only a month for the news to get out.

Just a month after that, in March, a San Francisco newspaper published a story stating that Samuel Brannan had rushed to set up a gold mining supply company. This was followed by another story claiming that there was gold in the American River. By August, newspapers on the other coast began reporting on the gold discovery, and by December President Polk confirmed there was gold out in California. As a result, thousands of East Coast residents headed west, joining immigrants who came to be known as "forty-niners" in rushing to California to get their share of the "Mother Lode" in Gold Country. Though Sutter's mill was ruined when his workers left to look for gold and squatters stole his cattle and supplies, his discovery launched one of the most famous periods in American history.

However, it was not all romanticized cowboys panning for gold and rushing across the horizon on horseback. In fact, it was a lawless land. Up until that point San Francisco had been a ghost town of closed businesses and abandoned homes with a population of just barely 1,000. Two years into the rush, the population reached 25,000. However, most land in California was under military control pending statehood. There was no civil legislature, no executive leader, and no judiciary. The "laws" were made up of a blend of Mexican and American statutes and common law.

Most miners operated on the "claim" principle that said so long as a claim was being worked by a prospector, it was his. This meant that they could not just stake a claim and then sit on it. When claims were abandoned, other miners could "claim-jump" and take control of them. The personal nature of the resulting disputes and their arbitration created ethnic divides between prospector groups, and as the influx of immigrants grew, regulations regarding maximum claim size followed.

As such rules were put in place, larger mining companies were established and mining technology improved. The West became ever more settled and developed as the desire for gold grew and grew. But California was not where the most interesting and unique gold hunt story took place. In the land east of California, in what's now the state of Arizona, the search for a fabled but never substantiated gold mine has been raging for years and continues to do so to this day. It's a good old-fashioned treasure hunt in the modern world, in a place where the mythologies of the local tribes and the beliefs of European immigrants blended together to create a land positively brimming with wonder and mystery. This place is called, rather poignantly, the Superstition Mountains.

Although California drew most of the attention and the prospectors, Arizona was also a fairly popular place to stake a claim. Unlike northern California, the winters in this area were mild, allowing prospectors to work year-round. On the other hand, the climate was arid and water was often in short supply. However, the potential rewards were high.

Long before the California Gold Rush, natives of the Arizona wilderness had been mining for precious metal, and it wasn't always gold. In fact, as early as 1000 BC, Native Americas began mining turquoise and copper which they used to make beautiful ornaments and decorations. The Apache tribes were known to mine cinnabar, an ingredient in their red body paint. When the Spanish conquistadors first came into contact with these tribes and took inventory of their jewelry, the modern mining industry started to take shape as the Spaniards hunted for their "three G's": glory, God, and gold. Throughout the 16th and 17th centuries, the Spanish set up settlements in the area, tried to convert the natives to the Catholic faith, and engaged in intermittent mining. However, the Apaches and Navajos proved to be less docile than the Spanish hoped, which created a dangerous situation for any European venturing out on a mining trip.

By 1850, the only real non-native settlement in the Arizona area was down south in Tucson. But the Spaniards had left enough of a legacy that many early Gold Rush era prospectors simply went out in search of old Spanish mines and laid claim to them in the hope that they might still pay out minerals. For those looking to create their own, still undiscovered wealth, the common practice was "placer" mining. This involved looking for the accumulation of minerals in stream beds and panning the sediment from the bottoms of rivers. Since it involved no excavation, it was a quick and cheap way to get started.

Civilization slowly followed on the heels of the renewed interest in the area, and in 1870 the first dwelling was built in the Phoenix area. At the same time, overnight settlements known as ghost towns began to pop up to provide shelter and sustenance for local prospectors. The largest dates to 1892, when mining for gold ore in the area was at a peak. The Mammoth Mine was the most prominent one in the vicinity, and it turned out a great deal of mineral before it ultimately flooded. It sits underwater to this day.

But the greatest legend of all comes from a mine that no one is entirely sure existed. Nevertheless, it has become an obsession for countless treasure hunters since the 19th century.

The Legend of the Superstitions

Arizona was always something of a mysterious place to those who came out west in search of land or gold or a new life under America's idea of Manifest Destiny. The land was arid and lacked the obvious basics for life. The flora looked dangerous and guarded its own water with sharp pricks and thorns on all sides. There was no true sign of green anywhere. The animals and insects that called this place home were dangerous and even deadly, quite ready to incapacitate or kill people who got too close. If the Christian minds of the East Coast ever envisioned a Hell on Earth, it probably looked a lot like Arizona.

But for the native tribes, this area was simply home, and had been for thousands of years. They were attuned to the environment and the terrain here and used the world around them to make lives for themselves. To them, this was no hell: It was their paradise. At least 22 separate tribes called Arizona home during the era before the European settlers arrived. Sadly, the story we're told of "how the West was won" often puts the natives in the role of villains and obstacles for hardy pioneers to overcome. But the lives of those who called this place home were real, and their world is never more present than when looking at the tales and beliefs of the Superstition Mountains.

The Superstition Mountains are a small range several miles east of downtown Phoenix. Just taking a look at the jagged rock of their peaks gives a feeling of wonder. The mountains look as though they pushed themselves straight up and out of the ground one day, uprooting the land and standing above the desert floor like a crown. Just one glance at the rough, strong profile cut into the horizon by the mountains give one a sense of wonder and an understanding as to why someone might call them the Superstitions. It's not surprising that the settlers in the area adopted many of the native beliefs about the mountains, which became blended with their own legends that developed as their community grew around the mountains.

Charles M. Skinner authored a total of nine volumes on the legends and myths of Native American tribes. One section dealt with the Superstition Mountains and the spirituality held by the Pima Indians of the area. The Pima (also known as the Akimel O'otham, or "river people") lived in southern Arizona for thousands of years. Their name, Pima, is believed to come from the phrase "I don't know" muttered in their native tongue when responding to questions from the first Spanish colonizers. After their initial contact with the colonists, the Pima were left to their own devices for much of the time until after the Mexican-American War, when their contact with Europeans became a constant.

One unique belief among the Pima is the sacredness of names. From childhood until marriage, children are not allowed to speak their own names lest it bring bad luck for their future. Speaking the names of the dead was believed to call upon their spirits and invoke bad luck as well.

When it came to the Superstition Mountains, they held a great number of mystic beliefs. Like many cultures throughout history, but somewhat ironically considering their arid desert homeland, the Pima people had their own version of the flood myth. They believed that Cherwit Make, the butterfly father of all animals, also made man when he sweated into the Salt River. As in many creation stories, man soon grew evil and violent. Cherwit Make warned them to live in peace and with honesty through a prophet named Suha. But the people did not listen, believing that Suha was simply a fool listening to the wind.

Suha, though, continued to insist that the creator of life would take that life away if they did not obey—and he was not the only one. The North Wind commanded the Pima people to turn to honesty with each other. The East Wind warned that the Sky Spirit would destroy all men. The West Wind also warned that evil would bring destruction on the Pima people. The South Wind whispered to Suha directly, telling him that he and his wife were going to be saved from the cataclysm. It ordered him to create a hollow bowl of spruce to live in during the flood.

Suha and his wife obeyed and watched from their safe haven as thunder and lightning rang out and the rain came down on the valley. Their spruce bowl landed on top of the Superstition Mountains during the storm, and after sleeping for a very long time they awoke to find that the floodwaters had cleared. It is said that the sharp outcroppings of rock at the top of the mountains are petrified Pima people who attempted to escape their fate by climbing to the summit.

Even then, the evil was not over. A devil named Hauk lurked in the Superstition Mountains, periodically venturing forth to steal daughters of the Pima tribe. One day, long after the flood, he stole Suha's own daughter. Suha followed them and watched as Hauk forced his daughter into servitude in the mountains. In retaliation, he poisoned the cactus wine that his daughter served to Hauk. The demon grew dizzy, and Suha beat him to death, freeing his daughter and the many missing girls stolen from the land.

However, it is believed that Hauk's spirit and anger still lurk in the mountains. It is also said that pieces of Hauk that broke off when Suha was beating him scattered throughout the land, becoming seeds of continued evil in man. Suha, in a final warning to his people, said that another flood would come to purge the world of the wicked. For that reason, the Pima were always reluctant to cross the Superstition Mountains. They also feared the anger of Cherwit Make, who resided there. Another legend states that the entrance to the underworld is situated on top of the mountains and the winds of the world originate from this portal.

A newer legend, likely created by European settlers, says that Geronimo is often seen going into the mountains and disappearing, only to turn up in New Mexico before coming back again. This gave rise to the fringe legend that the mountains contain a secret network of subterranean tunnels. The legend goes on to say that supernatural creatures inhabit the tunnels and there is a massive underground city and staircases that lead down into the very center of the Earth. It's easily the most hyperbolic legend about the place, but it's certainly a fun one to tell first-time hikers in the mountains—who then have to keep an eye out for a dark and mysterious cave that could be the entrance to the underworld!

These legends were well established by the time the gold rushers headed out West and walked into this land of wonder and mystery. The mountains cast their shadow on those who lived nearby, watching with awe the rocky faces staring down on the valley below. They created a romantic and Gothic image of the Southwest that we don't often get in the stories of gunslingers and train raids.

But one legend that originated in the era of gold and prospecting has made its mark on the area's mythos. It is this story that turned the Superstition Mountains from a local oddity of the Phoenix area to an internationally famous mystery. That is the sordid, complicated, oft-repeated, and still undead tale of the Lost Dutchman's Gold Mine.

The Dutchman and his Mine

The story of this mine begins long before the eponymous Dutchman (who was actually German) ever set foot in the United States. Archeological evidence and historic accounts prove that there was gold in the foothills of the Superstitions. However, some have asked whether this particular mine was actually a gold mine at all. While there was undoubtedly gold in the area, some think it unlikely that there could have been a substantial amount at the location described by the Dutchman and the treasure map on the Peralta stones (which we'll go into in more detail later).

Some claim that, instead of a mine, the Lost Dutchman's Gold Mine is rather a cache of gold collected from other mines. This story seems to jive well with the geological evidence that the described region could not support a substantial gold mine. It also reflects one of the early stories associated with the mine before it came into the possession of the Dutchman. However, the Lost Dutchman's Gold Mine has a lot more of a ring to it than Gold Cache, and so the legend of the mine is the one that persisted. In the remainder of this book, that's how we'll refer to this claimed cavern of riches, believed to be the largest deposit of gold in the Americas.

The story begins with the Peralta family of Mexico. According to legend, this rich and respected aristocratic family from Mexico came into the area in hopes of staking a gold claim during the gold rush out in California. What they found not only added to their wealth but angered the local Apache tribe. During a routine trip into the desert in 1848 to transport loot from the mine back to their estate in Mexico, the Peralta party came under attack from Apaches. A few members of the family escaped, but the gold was stolen and buried by the Apaches. The Peralta family was then cut off from their gold mine by fear of further attacks. Many contest the accuracy of this story, but it carries such weight with locals and treasure hunters that a trail and several geological features are named for the historic event. They include Massacre Falls and Massacre Grounds, which are located along Superstition hiking trails.

The massacre eventually led to the aforementioned Dutchman assuming ownership of the mine, but one more significant event happened first. Several years after the massacre one Dr. Thorne of the U.S. Army volunteered to treat a wounded Apache. The man turned out to be an important tribal leader, and he rewarded the doctor with treasure. The Apaches blindfolded Dr. Thorne and took him through the desert and into a cave. There, they removed his blindfold and allowed him to take as much gold as he could carry out with him. He was then deposited back in town. Dr. Thorne was unwilling to break the Apaches' trust by trying to locate the mine, but three soldiers of his acquaintance did set off into the desert to search for it. They apparently found something, because when they returned to town they boasted about a rich gold cache and showed off their treasure. But when they went back out, they never returned—killed perhaps by the elements, by the Apaches, or by jealous and greedy rivals for the gold.

Meanwhile, the Peraltas understandably wanted to sell their land in the Superstitions. Enter Jacob Waltz. Unlike many parts of the story, this one is factually accurate, verifiable by documentation. Jacob Waltz, the man who would go down in history as the Lost Dutchman, was a real person, born in Oberschwandorf in southern Germany in 1808. According to immigration records, he came to America in the mid-19th century and immediately went west looking for gold. In 1847, in the midst of his travels, he filed for naturalization. He arrived in the Phoenix area in the 1860s, purchased land from the Peralta family, and began coming into town with gold and tales of a rich vein on his new land out in the desert. Several people followed him into the desert, only to go missing.

Waltz's prosperity, however, was cut short by a devastating flood in 1891. The flood destroyed Waltz's farm, and the dampness resulted in a fatal case of pneumonia. He was looked after by Julia Thomas in his last days. He left her with a cryptic map that would, he said, eventually lead her to his mine out in the desert. Waltz died that October, and there are reports in local newspapers from September of the following year that Thomas and a band of partners were attempting to find his mine based on the clues he left. They came up empty, eventually selling the map for $7 to someone who wanted to try his own luck at the hunt for the Lost Dutchman's Gold Mine.

The Dutchman's boasting allowed the story and the notoriety of the mountains to live on throughout the ages, with the legend only growing as time went by. We have no idea what became of the map Thomas received from Waltz on his death bed and later sold for $7, though we're fairly certain no one found what they were looking for. (If they did, they were smart enough not to say anything about it.) However, a number of other maps have popped up since.

The Peralta Stones are a set of engraved stone slabs with odd markings that many believe to be a treasure map. They consist of two red sandstone tables and a red quartz rock cut into the pattern of a heart. The blocks are roughly 8¼ inches long, 5½ inches wide and ¾ of an inch thick. Inside one of the stones is a heart-shaped relief that fits the quartz heart perfectly. Across the slabs are lines and dots, including one long line. When the slabs are placed together with the stone heart insert, 18 dots are visible throughout the long line. The numbers and markings on the stone relief are thought to reveal the map's scale. Cryptic as it seems today, patterns of this type were actually used as maps during the Mexican-American War, when they were known as post road maps. However, the Peralta Stones themselves are somewhat shrouded in mystery. We're not sure who found the stones and we're not even sure when, although most agree it was sometime between 1949 and 1956.

The stones are on display in the Lost Dutchman Museum in Apache Junction, just outside Superstition State Park. Images of the stones have also been available on the internet for years. Quite a few people have made trips into the desert based on their interpretations of the Peralta Stones, and some believe they have gotten close to the treasure. In 2007, for example, two brothers from Apache Junction claimed to have located an old cave that was the entrance to the Lost Dutchman's Gold Mine. But these investigations have not been without cost, as we shall see in the next chapter.

Death in the Superstitions

Adolph Ruth was a treasure hunter who was possibly the biggest reason the world kept its attention on the Lost Dutchman's Gold Mine throughout the 20th century and into the 21st. The story of what happened to him in the 1930s sparked imagination and fear and resulted in decades of hunting in the desert to discover what he found—or at least discover what led to his untimely demise in the dangerous wilds of the Arizona. Of Ruth's life prior to the incident that would make the Superstition Mountains famous, we know very little. He was an amateur treasure hunter who enjoyed hiking through nature, and he had had some success in the past with locating old mines and buried troves. So, naturally, the rumors of the gold mine in his own backyard were too good to pass up.

The story begins with Adolph's son, Erwin C. Ruth. The younger Ruth was a lawyer in the town who at one point provided legal advice to a local man named Pedro Gonzalez. We don't know the details, but it seems that Erwin managed to keep the man out of jail, and for that Gonzalez was incredibly thankful. So thankful—or perhaps just so broke—that his payment for Erwin's services was a treasure map to the Peralta mine. Gonzalez claimed that he was descended from the Peralta family and had acquired the map as a family heirloom. Erwin passed the information along to his father, a known adventurer and mine hunter. Adolph had previously gone exploring in the Pegleg Mine out in California, and his expedition had resulted in a leg injury that would have kept a sane person out of the wilderness for good. But Ruth was not to be deterred by the pins in his leg—or the cane he needed to walk.

In the scorching heat of June 1931, Adolph Ruth set out into the wilderness, armed with the map and everything Gonzalez knew about the fabled mine in the mountains. He spent several days at a ranch owned by Tex Barkley, and his host urged him to abandon his quest due to the punishing summer weather and the incredibly rough terrain he would face if he followed the path the map laid out up and into the mountains. The sixty-six-year-old man ignored this advice and headed out on what was to be a two-week journey into the wilderness. Two weeks passed and he did not return. A search party was sent out after a few days, but nothing was found of Adolph Ruth.

The story died quickly. Fatalities were hardly uncommon in the Arizona wilderness, and it was assumed that the elderly Ruth had been claimed by an accidental fall, the sting of a scorpion, or maybe a rabid coyote. More optimistically, there was an outside chance that he had managed to avoid starvation and dehydration and was still lost in the wild. The summer passed and so did the fall. It was not until December of that year, six months after Ruth set out on his two-week expedition, that evidence of what happened to him finally turned up. The skull of a human male was found along the path that he'd been planning to take. Dr. Ales Hrdlicka, a respected anthropologist, examined the skull, photographs of Ruth, and Ruth's dental records to determine that it belonged to him. But that is far from all Dr. Hrdlicka discovered about the skull. He also identified two holes in the side that he believed were made by a shotgun or high-powered rifle fired at point-blank range. He identified clear entry and exit wounds and concluded that someone had shot Ruth. It was a chilling discovery and accusation to make.

Things only got worse. The following month, January 1932, search parties went out to recover Ruth's body. They found dismembered and scattered remains that they identified as Ruth's due to the plethora of personal items found with the decaying body parts. The metal pins from his injured leg were also used as identifying markers, leaving no doubt that these remains belonged to Adolph Ruth. Ruth's pistol was also found, fully loaded and with no sign of having been fired. What *wasn't* found in this pile of personal items was the Peralta map his son had given him before he went out on the expedition.

The picture painted by this evidence is a fairly clear one, but that didn't stop authorities from ruling the death a suicide. There are, of course, two obvious objections to that theory. First, how could Ruth shoot himself dead and then remove his own head and place it far away from the rest of his body? And even if coyotes or other scavengers dismembered his corpse, how could he have shot himself in the first place when all the bullets were left in his gun?

But even if authorities had opened a murder investigation, they would never have closed it. No suspects were ever identified, nor did anyone ever come forward with knowledge of Ruth's death. The enduring mystery launched the Superstition Mountains and their fabled gold mine into the consciousness of the wider world, but unfortunately, Ruth's was not the only death in the mountains.

Perhaps the most shocking thing about Ruth's death—beyond the unaccounted-for bullet holes and the missing map—was the fact that his head had been purposefully severed from his body and then removed from the rest of his remains. Perhaps a clever killer had wanted to reduce the chance of Ruth being identified. But his body was left on a rocky mountain trail used so infrequently that it was only stumbled upon six months later. The killer probably wasn't all that worried about the corpse ever being found. So was it ceremonial? Was it to just make incredibly sure that Ruth was dead?

Whatever the reason, Ruth was not the only person to end up headless on an excursion in search of the mine. One James A. Cravey was found in a similar manner just about 14 years after Ruth's demise. His headless remains were discovered in a canyon after he was reported missing after embarking on an expedition to find the mine in the mountains.

The deaths that would follow, and the mysterious manner in which they occurred, would inspire author Barry Storm to pen a book painting them as a murders committed to protect the mine.

Barry Storm, like many of the figures in our story, was a treasure hunter specializing in rummaging through old mines. In 1943, he began penning a series of articles for magazines and other periodicals about mining and backpacking in the desert. He also began to compile information into books that he would periodically rerelease as new facts became available, constantly updating his findings. His most famous work was *Thunder Gods Gold*, a book he updated and revised several times. One notable claim in Storm's book is that while he was exploring the Superstition Mountains he was almost killed by a sniper he referred to as "Mr. X". Storm postulated that Mr. X was a guardian of the Lost Dutchman's Gold Mine and had probably accounted for Cravey and Ruth years before.

Thunder Gods Gold was so popular that it inspired a full-length film, *Lust for Gold*, released in 1949. However, Storm wasn't a fan of the movie; he filed a lawsuit claiming that it damaged his reputation and misused his source material. Ultimately, though, his stories reached enough people that the legend persists.

And stories of this nature continued. Jesse Capen went missing in 2009 while hiking in the Tonto National Forest at the edge of the Superstition Mountains. His friends and family stated that he had become obsessed with the stories of the mine and had been trying to locate it for years. His body was not discovered until three years later when a search and rescue organization found his remains wedged into a crevice. In the meantime, Utah hikers Malcolm Meeks, Ardean Charles, and Curtis Merworth went missing in the mountains in 2010. They also were said to be looking for the mine. Their remains were found in 2011, long after the search had been called off and they had been presumed dead.

So, is there something guarding the mountains, or is it just a lot of inexperience and bad luck on the part of hikers throughout the years? Storm believed that this Mr. X tried to kill him while he was searching the mountains for the mine; did he succeed in murdering the others whose bodies were found there?

One of the earliest accounts of a man going missing in the mountains was that of Elisha Reavis, who was dubbed the "Madman of the Superstitions" and lived near the mountains in a secluded area until 1896, when his remains were found partially ravaged by coyotes. Notably, his head had been severed from his body and dragged several feet away.

In 1900 two prospectors known to history only as Silverlock and Malm were looking into a claim on the northern side of the mountain. They came across small amounts of gold but did not continue to work the site. In 1910, Malm showed up at a Mormon co-op in Mesa, where he began babbling incoherently that his partner had tried to kill him. Both men were brought into custody and deemed insane. They spent the rest of their lives in an institution.

In the late 1920s there was an unknown assailant who would send boulders down a cliff at hikers. A young boy visiting from New Jersey had his leg crushed by a boulder that had been tossed off the cliff at him. About a year later, two deer hunters were driven off the mountain when large rocks came cascading down on them. In 1937, a prospector by the name of Guy Fink came down off the mountain with some gold to show for his work. Just months later, his body was found on the side of a trail. He'd been shot in the stomach. His death was officially ruled an accident.

Another shooting that was ruled accidental involved Dr. John Burns from Oregon, who in 1951 was also found in the wilderness with a bullet wound as the apparent cause of death. In 1952, Joseph Kelley from Ohio was hiking in the mountains and never returned. Two years after he disappeared, his remains were found. The cause of death was a bullet hole in the top of his skull. The shot appeared to have been fired straight down from above. This too was ruled an accident. In 1956, a man reported his brother missing after he went looking for the mine up in the Superstition Mountains. His body was located a month later with a bullet hole in the head. A gun was found wedged beneath his body on the ground, and the authorities ruled his death a suicide.

In 1960, another headless skeleton was found near the foot of a cliff by a group of hikers. They alerted authorities who, four days later, identified it as the body of Franz Harrier, an Austrian student who had been visiting the area. There was no official cause of death. Only days later, the body of William Harvey was also found; again the cause of death was unknown.

Two prospectors, Hilmer Charles Bohen and Walter J. Mowry, were found dead in 1961. Bohen was buried in the sand with a bullet hole in his back. Mowry was located two months later in Needle Canyon, also shot to death. Jay Clapp had put in over a decade of prospecting work up in the Superstition Mountains before his body was discovered, without its head, in 1964. His head was never located, and his identity was only established by the initials scratched into the cameras that were found with him.

Some of these deaths seem to have obvious explanations. Lack of experience and lack of preparation in the Superstition wilderness could kill even the hardiest of explorers, so many of these deaths could be attributed to natural causes: exhaustion, starvation, dehydration. Some could be attributed to missteps and falls in the notoriously rough mountain terrain that hikers must pass through. But some deaths are not so easy to explain away. The number of deaths by gunshot wound is astounding, and the location and trajectory of the bullets in many of these cases makes it impossible for them to be suicides—not to mention Adolph Ruth, whose bullets were all left inside his gun, despite the point-blank bullet holes in the side of his skull!

There have always been rumors and theories about exactly what happened to these people, and many more have popped up since the internet opened the floodgates for treasure hunters to communicate across the world in real time. Some work together in an attempt to make sense of the stories and come to a common understanding about the legends and their possible truth. Others have more outlandish theories about how and why people go missing in the mountains while looking for treasure.

A group known to believers as "The Black Legion" are said to be the guardians of the gold and the secrets of the mountains. They are believed to be a secret organization of possibly Apache warriors, dressed in black, who have guarded the location of the this mine or cache of gold since the days of Dr. Thorne's visit to the mysterious treasure cave. Supposedly they also funnel gold to and from their secret location as needed and have been known to take out those who get in their way or threaten their ability to move and guard their gold. It is believed that they are the ones responsible for the beheadings in the mountains.

Is it true? Who can say. The possibility of a secret organization always pops up when the world has questions about mysteries. This mystery is no different. A rash of unexplained deaths haunted the area, and when the authorities could not explain it, residents came up with their own theories. Ultimately, the story will probably be lost to history—unless more mysterious deaths occur, in which case it will no doubt evolve as the facts grow and change.

Directions to the Lost Dutchman's Gold Mine

If you think you're mentally up to the task of researching, and physically up to the task of searching the Superstition Mountains yourself (after rigorous training and preparation, as the many stories of untimely deaths will warn you), then here are the clues the Lost Dutchman has left us to follow. It's a treasure map straight out of a pirate story. It's confusing, and given that so many people have tried and failed to find any treasure with it, quite possibly completely fictitious. But for the hardiest out there, here are the clues to follow if you find yourself one day ready to take on the quest:

1. It lies within an imaginary circle whose diameter is not more than five miles and whose center is marked by Weaver's Needle, about 2,500 feet high, among a confusion of lesser peaks and mountainous masses of basaltic rock. On the south side of the west end of the range is a trail which leads northward over a lofty ridge, thence downward past Sombrero Butte into a long canyon running north, and finally to a tributary canyon very deep and rocky and densely wooded with a continuous thicket of scrub oak. Then up the side canyon past water. It's about 200 feet across from a cave.

2. If you pass three red hills you have gone too far.

3. You can watch the military trail from the mine, but you cannot be seen from the military trail.

4. The setting sun shines through a break in the mountains and glitters upon the ore and shaft.

5. You have to climb a short ways from a steep ravine in order to see Weaver's Needle to the southward from above the mine.

6. You can see Weaver's Needle to the south and Four Peaks to the north. From this vantage Four Peaks looks like one peak.

7. From the cave you go about a mile up the same canyon, which runs north-south, until you find a ridge upon the end of which is a natural stone face looking upward to the east. Directly across from the face is a high narrow ravine where you will find the inclined entrance to the mine. Down the slope below the mine shaft is a walled up tunnel. The canyon can be identified further by the tumbled ruins of an old Spanish-built stone house near its head.

8. There is a roofless two-room house made of heaped up stones in the mouth of a large cave near the mine. The cave is near the bottom of a high bluff and faces northward. You need to hang a tarpaulin in the entrance to keep out of the north wind and rain.

9. The shaft goes down along an eighteen-inch vein of rose quartz which is studded with pinhead nuggets of gold. Beside it, a three-inch hanging wall of hematite quartz is composed of about one-third pure gold.

10. The first gorge is on the south side of the west end of the range. There the trail is marked northward over a lofty ridge. Then it goes past a high pinnacle of rock into a long canyon running north, and finally through a tributary canyon which is very deep and rocky. Traces of mining operations are to be found on the southern slope of the

mountain in front of a hat-shaped hill at the entrance to the canyon of willows. Nearby are the ruins of a stone adobe house and a half buried stone monument.

11. Start from the first natural stone face near the western end of the mountains. From the direction of approach over the desert you have to go up the first deep canyon from the western end of the range. Then climb northward over the backbone of the mountains until you come within sight of a huge, sombrero-shaped peak. Travel downward past the base of this sombrero into a long canyon running north until you find on the east side a tributary canyon which is very deep, pot-holed, and densely wooded with scrub oak. Then turn about and go back southward up this tributary canyon until you reach a point where the outline on the horizon matches the outline on the map. Go up a steep tributary arroyo which seems to run right into the shadows of overhanging cliffs, but instead ends finally in a miniature hidden valley. The gold shaft is in this valley.

12. In a gulch in the Superstition mountains, the location of which is described by certain landmarks, there is a two-room house in the mouth of a cave on the side of a slope near the gulch. About 200 yards across the gulch, opposite this house in the cave, is a tunnel, which will be covered up and concealed in the bushes. Here is the mine, the richest in the world. Some distance above the tunnel on the side of the mountain is a shaft or incline. It is steep but possible to climb down. This is carefully covered. The shaft goes right down into the midst of a rich gold ledge where the gold can be picked off in big flakes.

13. Go to First Water, then to Second Water, then take the old government trail to San Carlos. Where the trail turns south, you will see over the point of the ridge. You can look north and see the Four Peaks lined up to look like one peak. In the other direction you will see a high, needle-pointed rock. In the canyon under you is the hidden camp. You can't get down there because it is too steep, so go to the mouth of the canyon and then back. You can find the rock house with very little difficulty. You won't be able to see it until you are right upon it. After finding the camp, come back out of the canyon. Across the canyon and up it is a side canyon. Go up this side canyon to a cave. Opposite the cave is a tunnel and the mine.

Further Readings

So, if you think you have what it takes, go ahead and take on the challenge and the legends of the Lost Dutchman's Gold Mine! You can use these resources for further research on the topic:

Thunder Gods Gold by Barry Storm: https://www.amazon.com/Thunder-Gods-Gold-Barry-Storm/dp/1478179929

Hiker's Guide to the Superstition Wilderness by Jack C. Carlson and Elizabeth Stewart https://www.amazon.com/Hikers-Guide-Superstition-Wilderness-Arizonas/dp/1884224059/ref=pd_sim_14_3?_encoding=UTF8&pd_rd_i=1884224059&pd_rd_r=JVWVNK407ZQDD46Q2DKA&pd_rd_w=GrRxP&pd_rd_wg=ScsPL&psc=1&refRID=JVWVNK407ZQDD46Q2DKA

Quest for the Dutchman's Gold: The 100-Year Mystery by Sobert Sikorksy https://www.amazon.com/Quest-Dutchmans-Gold-100-Year-Superstition/dp/0914846566/ref=pd_sim_14_7?_encoding=UTF8&pd_rd_i=0914846566&pd_rd_r=539E2B31ECVT4RJP2PY5&pd_rd_w=gq6FT&pd_rd_wg=DHVmb&psc=1&refRID=539E2B31ECVT4RJP2PY5

The Story of the Superstition Mountain and the Lost Dutchman Gold Mine by Robert Joseph Allen https://www.amazon.com/Story-Superstition-Mountain-Lost-Dutchman/dp/0671814303/ref=pd_sim_14_6?_encoding=UTF8&pd_rd_i=0671814303&pd_rd_r=JXMXAC16K253DHD7RFYQ&pd_rd_w=T2ULA&pd_rd_wg=XLt4J&psc=1&refRID=JXMXAC16K253DHD7RFYQ

Treasure Expeditions:
http://treasureexpeditions.com/clues_lost_dutchman_gold_mine_bradley_brad_williamson.htm

Lost Dutchman Goldmine forums: http://www.thelostdutchmangoldmine.com/

Made in the USA
Columbia, SC
01 July 2024

37949429R00020